# THE COST OF ABORTION

An Analysis of the Social, Economic, and
Demographic Effects of Abortion
in the United States.

Lawrence F. Roberge

Foreword by Suzanne M. Rini
Afterword by James McGregor

Printed in the United States of America

Library of Congress Catalog Card Number: 95-61930

ISBN: 1-885857-16-0

Four Winds
PO Box 3102
LaGrange, GA 30241
Editing, Layout
Emily Rose Eldredge

For Book Orders Call:
1-800-552-1098
Fax 706-882-7999

# ENDORSEMENTS

"Lawrence Roberge is to be commended for gathering together in one place such a broad range of abortion-related data. He suggests possible connections between abortion and many harmful medical, social, and economic trends in society. These connections must now be further investigated. In light of Roberge's analysis, they can not simply be ignored."

**- Dr. John F. Kilner, Ph.D., Director, The Center for Bioethics and Human Dignity.**

"L.F. Roberge's The Cost of Abortion proves that our United States can not afford this willful waste of human lives by abortion. Every serious speaker on life issues must read this book."

**- Dr. Mildred F. Jefferson, M.D., Assistant Clinical Professor of Surgery, Boston University School of Medicine and President, Right to Life Crusade.**

"I want to see this book in the hands of EVERY Catholic priest and Protestant minister in the country so they can preach the truth of this book from the pulpit."

**-Father Tom DeLorenzo, Host, In Season and Out of Season Radio Program.**

# DEDICATION

To Manuel Antonio Goncalves Jr.,
Alexander Joseph Goncalves,
and Sarah Elizabeth Roberge

May they live in a world free from the cost of abortion.

# ACKNOWLEDGMENTS

I would like to thank those who have demonstrated their support and encouragement through out this project: Donna and Manny Sr. Goncalves, Connie Roberge (mom), Danny and Barbara Roberge, Lisa Zajac, Tim and Tammy Biggins, Bruce and Bev Murch, Ken Johnson, Paul Desilets, Judy Rice, Eleanor Rae, Dr. James McGregor, Peter Biggins, Rev. Skip Robokoff, Frank Kelly, Betty Slaney, and Pam Levy. Special thanks goes to Atty. Gregory Hession for reviewing and providing helpful feedback; Mr. Richard Pasquini for providing education references; and to Ms. Joyce Farrell for reviewing, encouragement, and direction. And much thanks goes to (of course!), Jesus Christ.

# FOREWORD

The <u>Roe vs. Wade</u> Supreme Court decision was framed around the alleged presence of a "penumbra" in the 14th Amendment. The penumbra welded a "right to privacy" with the act of abortion. This framework resulted in abortion being excised from its historical identity as eugenics, made it solely a private matter devoid of eugenical implications, and excised it from any constellation of considerations such as its physical and psychiatric sequelae, its relationship to economics and to other matters of national import, the framework of <u>Roe</u> then became an envelope of denial of historical verities and of consequences.

The dominant voices in the beleaguered abortion debate have coalesced around their respective slogans, "the right to choose", and "the right to life". Sole emphasis on the rights of women and the humanity and the rights of the unborn have then also excluded a wider framework being applied to abortion's impact. Those for "a right to choose" must by necessity of raising "choice" to an <u>a priori</u> status, deny the realm of consequence. Those who solely emphasize the unborn's right to life and their humanity see in the matter of consequences a degradation of their primary focus on the baby, as well as a dangerous flirtation with the doctrine of proportionalism, an offbrand but popular theologism which entails defining the good or evil of acts by their outcomes. Yet, there does exist for abortion a wider purview...a mightily objective one. Mr. Roberge has alighted upon it. With the unemotional and impervious mind of an expert scientist and technician, he has scoured the available data and then subjected it to the cold embrace of analysis. The pleasure or displeasure of one or another audience is not his concern.

With the present study, Mr. Roberge joins other most welcome researchers and writers who lately have gone into the very interesting areas of demographics to find the human and political impact of changed reproductive behavior. For instance, Richard A. Soloway, in 1990 contributed <u>Demography and Degeneration: Eugenics and the Declining Birthrate in Twentieth Century England</u> (1). Mr. Soloway's work chronicling the relationship between widespread practice of birth control in response to eugenics and population control ideology is vindicated by a vast bibliography that proves the necessity of this sort of study. Then there is British scholar, Paul Weindling's, <u>The Sonderweg of German Eugenics, Nationalism and Internationalism</u> (2). It also verifies the distinct relationship between the Germans tendency toward birth control and the rise of eugenics in Germany, mainly through the economic appeal. Presently, Mr. Roberge, although his framework does not mention eugenics, produces material that coalesces with the works just cited and those in the same constellation. Those few of us writers staked out on the eugenics theme understand the trajectory of Mr. Roberge's tables and charts and are grateful for his doing that part of the work which our own expertise can not.

Mr. Roberge has also done much to provide a level playing field, too long occupied only by demographers from the population control camp, who see abortion as one means among many — contraception, sterilization, and phrases such as "sustainable development" — to reduce population. Because of its ideological agenda, this powerful community has not provided data reflective of any "cost" of abortion, not of its historically proven relationship to eugenics, not to any deteriorative effects on the health and fertility of women, not to the economic stability of the nation. As readers of Mr. Roberge's work shall clearly see by his summoning of data from so many diverse sources and then from his ensuing analysis, the "cost" of abortion is both real and high.

It is undeniable that the decriminalization of abortion appeared in the United States when there were two major cultural groups who saw abortion in terms of their own ideological agendas, namely the youth culture with its emphasis on "sexual revolution" and the feminist one which made abortion its working icon of its version of "woman's liberation". However, these communities do not have the vitality nor the following they once did. Nor will they have to confront the long-term "cost" of abortion for the next generation. Thus, it is well that Mr. Roberge has put his diverse talents to the wheel of objective data at this particular juncture in time. The new generation can study his results, and forge a consensus based upon it. There is no logical or humane reason to keep from the new generation the "cost of abortion", since they will be the ones inheriting the downside of those costs.

The great range of public officials should find Mr. Roberge's work especially liberating, its methodology and presentation free them of the "hot potato" nature of abortion politics. For instance, public health officials can not, unless they wish to risk professional suicide, afford to turn a blind eye to Mr. Roberge's data on Asherman's Syndrome, a medical sequela of abortion accounting for an upswing in female infertility. The issue of abortion meets the demand for the public's right to know, with the public official of many types being the accountable link between the two. Politicians who daily toil over the seemingly mystical sciences of economics and the national debt, as with the all too knowable factors of goods in production vs. consumption and of the GDP, will be astounded to find, at long last, that the hidden quotient of abortion impinges upon all of these matters. Guided by Mr. Roberge's pioneering effort, others skilled in the same disciplines will be encouraged to look at even more areas, using abortion as the vector of their searches and analysis. It is exciting at last to find that abortion is linked to so many vital signs. And this linkage does very much bring home that the extinguishing of the life of one human being brings with it a domino effect tracing back to the fact that as reproduction goes, so goes humanity and its institutions. OR, as George Elliot wrote, "There is no private life which is not determined by a wider public life."

> Suzanne M. Rini
> Journalist and Author
> Pittsburgh
> May 27, 1995

References:

1.     Soloway, Richard. 1990. Demography and Degeneration, Eugenics and the Declining Birthrate in Twentieth Century Britain. Chapel Hill and London: The University of North Carolina Press.

2.     Weindling, P., The Sonderweg of German Eugenics, Nationalism, and Internationalism. British Journal of the History of Science. 22, part 3 of 74, Sept. 1989.

# PROLOGUE
## ABORTION
# IS THERE A COST TO SOCIETY?

The debate over abortion in American society continues to rage. Both sides (pro-life and pro-choice) claim to have the upper hand, both philosophically and politically. Both sides clamor with facts, figures, opinion polls, and graphic details.

The purpose of this publication is to investigate whether any indications exist that legalized abortion has (or will have) an effect on the United States as a society. This publication was NOT designed for theological discourses, civil or constitutional rights arguements, or philosophical debates, as many publications exist on these topics. Granted, I have heard many views that the societal infrastructure (the soul of the nation) has been harmed by abortion. Cries arise that human life is cheapened by the legalization of abortion (1). Rhetoric exists that the constitutional right to privacy includes abortion; therefore the right to an abortion is a constitutionally protected right (2). A short, yet intelligent, review of the historical and legal issues involving the legalization of abortion in the U.S. is covered by Flanders (2).

Furthermore, I have heard about the effects caused by abortion from friends, neighbors, religious, etc. For example: many argue that abortion causes reduced population growth rates, less available adoptions, slowed economic growth, etc.. **BUT, hearing these quotes is one thing; finding the facts to back these quotes is another!** That is the purpose of this research.

I wished to obtain the facts and data that would refute or substantiate the claims that abortion affects various aspects of U.S. society. It is my hope that this composition will contribute to intelligent debate regarding abortion in the marketplace of ideas.

I have analyzed data from 1965 to 1990 (or 1992 when I could locate it). Where I could find indications to support a supposition, I have tried to provide graphs or tables or both for easy comprehension. These vehicles are distilled from data collected from a variety of sources and these sources are cited for the readers further review. I refused to accept data for which I could not cite the source. For the reader, I have simplified the analysis and the presentation to include an introduction, graphic/table, discussion, and an end section conclusion. Also, I have tried to flag the most salient points for those with short attention spans.

There is a familiar saying known to students of statistics, "That correlation does not indicate causality.". In several of the chapters (i.e. Chapters 7,8,9), correlation between abortion numbers and Gross Domestic Product, Personal Income, and tax revenues denote an association (i.e. a "possible", but NOT definite relationship). But, as all good statisticians will note, an association is not the same as causation (a direct measurable relationship). I include reasoning to support the association between abortion numbers and economic factors (and true to scientific form, I mention other factors of influence other than abortion). However, evidence for a solid conclusive causation between these factors may require several decades of data before causation can be deduced. As for the causality of other relationships (population growth, births, education, fertility rates, etc.) with abortion, these are more clearly and scientifically evident at present.

The first section is very important, as it reviews basic abortion statistics. It also demonstrates the confusion over abortion statistics due to varying statistical sources and the methods of collecting the data. This is a very important point as the data overwhelmingly indicates that the total number of U.S. abortions (both yearly and cumulative) are HIGHER than ANY source has counted!

For those intimidated by tables of data (or just wanting to extract information more effectively!), I encourage you to use a ruler or similar straightedge. Follow along the tables, line by line, and you will be able to compare the numbers more effectively. Notice differences horizontally (EXAMPLE: compare CDC's data with AGI's data in Table 1.1) and vertically (EXAMPLE: compare 1977 and 1978 student enrollment figures in Table 6.2). I believe this method will help anyone new to reading tables of numbers to be able to fully appreciate the information in this book. Also, DO NOT PANIC! I have tried to mention in the text those critical points that show up in the tables and graphs. The purpose of this book was to get the information to the non-scientific reader (AND have them understand it!).

Due to the approximately 20 years of abortion data, I am limited to covering five basic topics: Basic Abortion Data; Births, Fertility Rates, and other Consequences; Population Growth; Education; and Early Economic/Fiscal Factors. I have also included a prologue discussion to review and provide a glimpse into possible future effects.

Lawrence F. Roberge M.S.

XIII

# CONTENTS

# LIST OF GRAPHS

# CHAPTER 1
# BASIC ABORTION FIGURES
# THE FIGURES ARE WRONG!

Remember all the abortion figures (i.e. statistics) quoted from the media, prochoice forces, prolife forces, and everyone else? No? Notice how confusing it can get? Is the total number of abortions 30 million or 28.7 million... or is it 25 million or 32 million?

This first chapter attempts to examine basic abortion figures as well as problems in obtaining an accurate count of the total abortions performed in the U.S.. Also, this section examines how different sources obtained their abortion data.

Also, this section examines the lesser known data concerning abortions performed prior to 1973. This pre-1973 data is important and will be useful in later comparisons with other social, economic, and demographic factors.

## BASIC ABORTION DATA

The first table (see Table 1.1), compares abortion statistical data from two primary (and much quoted) sources, The Alan Guttmacher Institute (AGI) and the Centers for Disease Control (CDC).

# THE COST OF ABORTION

## Table 1.1-COMPARISON OF AGI AND CDC ABORTION STATISTICS; BOTH YEARLY AND CUMULATIVE.

| Year | Annual Abortion Figures-AGI | Cumulative Abortion Figures-AGI | Annual Abortion Figures-CDC | Cumulative Abortion Figures-CDC |
|---|---|---|---|---|
| 70 | | | 193,491 | 193,491 |
| 71 | | | 485,816 | 679,307 |
| 72 | | | 586,760 | 1,266,067 |
| 73 | 744,610 | 744,610 | 615,831 | 1,881,898 |
| 74 | 890,570 | 1,643,180 | 763,476 | 2,645,374 |
| 75 | 1,034,170 | 2,677,350 | 854,853 | 3,500,227 |
| 76 | 1,179,300 | 3,856,650 | 988,267 | 4,488,494 |
| 77 | 1,316,700 | 5,173,350 | 1,079,430 | 5,567,924 |
| 78 | 1,409,600 | 6,582,950 | 1,157,776 | 6,725,700 |
| 79 | 1,497,570 | 8,080,520 | 1,251,921 | 7,977,621 |
| 80 | 1,553,890 | 9,634,410 | 1,297,606 | 9,275,227 |
| 81 | 1,577,340 | 11,211,750 | 1,300,760 | 10,575,987 |
| 82 | 1,573,920 | 12,785,670 | 1,303,980 | 11,879,967 |
| 83 | 1,575,000 | 14,360,670 | 1,268,987 | 13,148,954 |
| 84 | 1,577,180 | 15,937,850 | 1,333,521 | 14,482,475 |
| 85 | 1,588,550 | 17,526,400 | 1,328,570 | 15,811,045 |
| 86 | 1,574,000 | 19,100,400 | 1,328,112 | 17,139,157 |
| 87 | 1,559,110 | 20,659,510 | 1,353,671 | 18,492,828 |
| 88 | 1,590,750 | 22,250,260 | 1,371,285 | 19,864,113 |
| 89 | 1,566,900 | 23,817,160 | 1,396,658 | 21,260,771 |
| 90 | 1,608,600 | 25,425,760 | 1,429,577 | 22,690,348 |
| 91 | 1,556,500 | 26,982,260 | | |
| 92 | 1,528,900 | 28,511,160 | | |

Source: AGI, CDC (3,4,39,40)

2

# BASIC ABORTION FIGURES: THE FIGURES ARE WRONG

The Centers for Disease Control (CDC) data (3,40) covers the period of 1970-1990, whereas the Alan Guttmacher Institute (AGI) data (4,39) covers the period of 1973-1992. The CDC Figures also include abortion data from the period 1970-72. The sum total of this period is almost 1.3 million abortions. These abortions occurred as some states legalized abortion laws prior to the 1973, U.S. Supreme Court Roe vs. Wade decision (2). This is an important point to remember, as it will relate to graphs and tables later in this text. Henceforth it will be referred to as the "70-72 series".

Although CDC Figures covers, a longer span of time, even the CDC report (3) concedes that its numbers are lower and less accurate than the AGI data. The reasoning stated in the report is that CDC data was supplied by central health agencies, whereas the AGI data was obtained by direct surveys of abortion providers.

Yet, even the AGI data is incomplete. A study by Henshaw and Van Hort (5), both from AGI, clearly states that they may have under surveyed the total number of abortion providers (and thereby under counted the total number of abortions) by 6.5 percent. This is due in part to overlooking small abortion providers such as physicians who perform abortions in their own offices or facilities that were resistant to release data for the study. The study states that a prior 1982 abortion survey may have understated the count and be short by 110,000 abortions. Thus, although the AGI data is closest to the real total number, in fact, it may be undercounting by approximately 6 percent. Therefore, the TRUE cumulative abortion numbers may be approximately 6 percent greater than reported! **Thus, even in the 1990's, true abortion statistics (both yearly and cumulative) may be 6 percent (or more) GREATER than ANY source can quote!**

3

Nevertheless, for most of the following studies, AGI data will be used, except in cases that require the 70-72 series to help fulfill the explanation.

The yearly increase of abortions is illustrated by Graph 1.1.

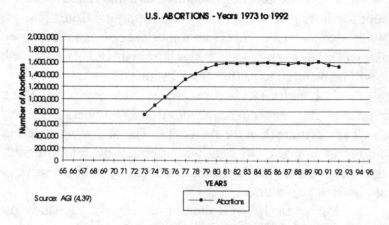

**GRAPH 1.1** - YEARLY U.S. ABORTIONS FOR 1973-1992.

This graph shows the yearly rise of abortions though the 1970's until a rough plateau occurs through the 1980's and into the 1990's. Note that this plateau signals that the velocity of abortions (i.e. the yearly increase) has ceased. Also, by 1992, it appears that a decline in yearly abortions has begun. Further studies during the 1990's are necessary to verify this emerging trend. **Simply put, the yearly growth rate of abortions has leveled off.**

A study by Henshaw and Van Vort (39) suggests several reasons why abortion numbers have leveled off the in the later 1980's and early 1990's. One reason is that by the early 1990's, the number of abortion providers has decreased. Also, the study cites pressure from prolife activism (e.g.

4

peaceful protests, sidewalk counseling, Operation Rescue-style clinic shutdowns, etc.) as another factor.

Cal Thomas (38) states that the reduction in abortion numbers is due to the proliferation of crisis pregnancy centers which provide women with an alternative to abortion.

To understand the cumulative effect of abortion (and to obtain a more accurate figure of total U.S. abortions), the cumulative effect of abortions is described in Graph 1.2. Note the steady increase from 1978 to 1992.

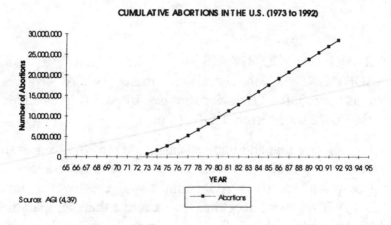

CUMULATIVE ABORTIONS IN THE U.S. (1973 to 1992)

Source: AGI (4,39)

**GRAPH 1.2** - CUMULATIVE U.S. ABORTIONS FOR 1973-1992.

Based on AGI data, from 1973 to 1992, the total number of abortions was 28,511,160.

Another clear example of the disparity between AGI and CDC abortion statistics is demonstrated in Graph 1.3.

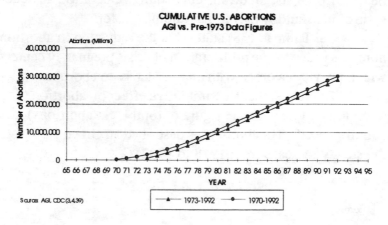

CUMULATIVE U.S. ABORTIONS
AGI vs. Pre-1973 Data Figures

Source: AGI, CDC (3,4,39)

1973-1992  •  1970-1992

**GRAPH 1.3** - COMPARISON OF CUMULATIVE U.S. ABORTIONS. Note the cumulative differences in AGI figures versus the modified figures composed of AGI figures added to the 70-72 series (from CDC) figures.

Notice that adding the totals from the 70-72 series to the AGI 1973-1992 figures results in a new cumulative abortion figure which exceeds the AGI cumulative figures, even though CDC 1970-1990 numbers are less accurate than comparable AGI data (see Table 1.2). Again, cumulative AGI will be referenced, except when the "70-72 series" data will be required to fulfill the correlational explanation.

Why is the "cumulative" abortion data important? It tells us the total number of abortions done over a period of time. This "missing population" will be an important concept in later chapters which examine the effects this missing population would have had on the economic growth, on population issues, and in education.

I must note that these statistics may only be the tip of the iceberg. The data supplied counts only surgically induced abortions. Dr. Bogomir Kuhar (31), pharmaceutical consultant and president of Pharmacists For Life, has examined and calculated out the number of U.S. abortions induced by all methods: surgical (e.g. D&C, instillation), mechanical (e.g. intrauterine device), and chemical (e.g. oral contraceptives, "morning after" pill). **He has estimated that there are between 9.6 to 13.4 million abortions occurring per year.** After reviewing Kuhar's study, the reader can understand the sheer complexity in determining the true number of abortions occurring in the United States!

In conclusion, the review of basic abortion data demonstrates the need to know the sources of abortion data and why the statistics may differ between studies. Based on AGI data, the total number of abortions from 1973 to 1992 is 28,511,160. If CDC data from 1970 to 1972 is included in the AGI data, then the total number rises to 29,777,227.

It is important to note that NO single study can completely guarantee an absolutely accurate count on the total number of abortions. Various factors contributed to problems with abortion surveys, including small abortion provider sites at physician offices; differing collection methods; and availability problems with the abortion data. Several studies (3,5) suggest that the total (yearly and cumulative) abortion figures exceed even AGI figures by perhaps 6 percent.

Also, the cumulative effect is important because it may demonstrate cumulative effects which can become detected over time.

Finally, CDC data, demonstrates that from 1970 to 1972, a total number of nearly 1.3 million abortions occurred in the United States. This may prove to be important for the further analysis of other trends in later chapters. This period will be referred to as the "70-72 series".

# CHAPTER 2
## ONE COST OF ABORTION
## LOWER BIRTH RATES!

This chapter examines whether abortion has effected the birth rate in the United States. The reader might ask, "Look, can you REALLY detect any change in the massive numbers of births versus the smaller numbers of abortions?".

Good question! The answer to that question is "Yes", as the data will show.

Although the U.S. birth rate has been declining since the first census in 1790 (with exception of the "baby boom" from 1947-1964), abortion may have further aggravated the drop in the birth rate (6).

Upon examination of total U.S. births (see Graph 2.1), one can note the decline starting in 1970 (perhaps due to the 70-72 series of abortions) which levels off during 1976.

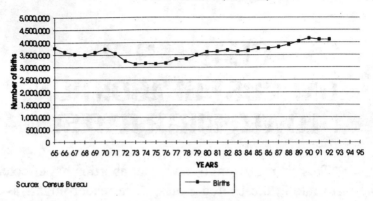

**GRAPH 2.1** - TOTAL U.S. BIRTHS FOR 1965-1992.

Also, note the steady but slow rise in the birth rate during the later 1970's and 1980's. Despite the slow rise in births in the late 1980's and early 1990's, this increase is not considered another "baby boom", but rather an "echo" of the prior baby boom (7,8). Furthermore, due in part to baby boomers having children and women who delayed childbearing until their 30's, the United States will not achieve a birth rate equal to the minimum population replacement level of 2.1 children (per woman). The Bureau of Census speculates that, at most, the "Birth Echo" will result in a birth rate of 1.9 children (per woman); far short of population replacement levels. As a consequence, our total population will decline, if PRESENT TRENDS continue.

This raises the question, "What would the birth rate be if the total births included the abortion numbers?" In reality, what would have been the birth rate if abortion had NOT terminated those pregnancies?

# ONE COST OF ABORTION: LOWER BIRTH RATES

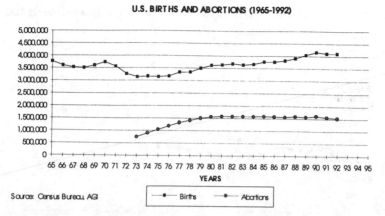

U.S. BIRTHS AND ABORTIONS (1965-1992)

Source: Census Bureau, AGI

**GRAPH 2.2** - COMPARISON OF YEARLY U.S. BIRTHS AND YEARLY U.S. ABORTIONS FOR 1965-1992

Comparing birth data with yearly AGI data (see Graph 2.2), one can observe similarities in the growth rates and plateaus of both births and abortions. Note that from 1980 till 1988, both curves appear to flatten out, indicating no growth. When abortion became legalized in 1973, its statistical growth may be related to the decline in the birth rate from 1973 to 1977. While abortion was steadily increasing, birth rate growth was weak. Finally as previously mentioned, the 70-72 series may help explain the beginning of the birth rate decline starting in the early 1970's.

The above data suggests that legalized abortions may have been a contributing factor in the reduced birth rates in the United States. Westoff (6) notes that illegitimate pregnancies in the 1950's and 1960's would normally be legitimatized by marriage, whereas in the more recent decades (1970's, 1980's, and 1990's), the tendency is to abort the pregnancy or have an out-of-wedlock birth.

To compare actual birth rates to the potential rate had

11

there been no abortion, we add abortion numbers to the yearly birth figures creating a number labeled "adjusted births" (see Graph 2.3).

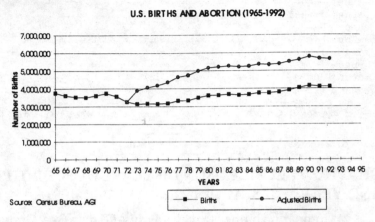

GRAPH 2.3 - COMPARISON OF U.S. BIRTHS WITH AND WITHOUT ADDED ABORTION NUMBERS. Note: adjusted births is the sum of the yearly U.S. births and yearly AGI abortion figures for that respective year.

Note in Graph 2.3 the effects on the growth of birth rates as abortion statistics are added. Note that the 70-72 series would have filled in the 1970-1972 gap in the birth data. Also, note that adding potential births as reflected in the abortion figures to actual births, the 1970's would have had a statistical growth in births (with subsequent effects on social and economic factors in U.S. society; everything from diaper and toy sales to school enrollment and car purchases. But more on that later!), with the 1980's and 1990's showing a leveling off of births in excess of 5 million yearly. This potential growth slope will be important in later chapters. There may have also been a secondary effect as a larger 1970's population reached child bearing age in the 1990's.

In conclusion, the data suggests that abortion has had a noticeable effect on birth rates in the United States. This decline in births can be detected in the early 1970's and therefore the 70-72 series can be useful to help support the relationship between abortions and the decline in births in the U.S.. Finally, when the abortion numbers are added to the birth numbers, the data suggests that the U.S. would have experienced a growth period throughout the 1970's and a steady plateau of over 5 million births per year throughout the 1980's and early 1990's. The economic and social effects from this absence of growth in births will be discussed in later chapters.

# CHAPTER 3
## ABORTION AND
## THE FERTILITY FACTOR

Another important variable to examine for the effects of abortion is the United States fertility rate. The term "fertility rate" describes a group's capacity to bear children. This information will be helpful for answering the following questions: Can the effects of abortion be detected in the national fertility rate? Does abortion actually cause a decline in the national fertility rate? Also, does abortion affect the fertility of individual women who obtain abortions? Remember, a decrease in individual fertility will reflect back on national fertility rates, but, this effect must be in large enough quantities to affect the national statistics!

By obtaining data from the National Center for Health Statistics, the following graph has been developed (see Graph 3.1).

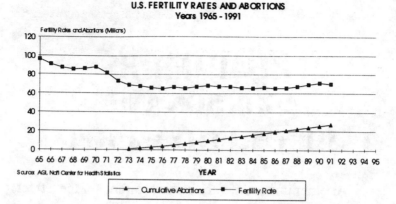

**GRAPH 3.1** - COMPARISON OF U.S. FERTILITY RATES AND YEARLY U.S. ABORTIONS. Note: fertility rates for U.S. women ages 15-44, and for all races.

Note that the figures in this graph are for women 15 to 44 years of age. The data demonstrates a decrease in the fertility rate when compared with the cumulative abortion curve. If the 70- 72 series is added, the drop in fertility rates coincide with the incidence and cumulative increase in abortions. The most significant effect on fertility rates is demonstrated by the near plateau effect during 1973-1988, which follows the AGI data of legalized abortions. Both Westoff (6) and Wattenberg (9) attribute legal abortion as a contributing factor in the decline of the U.S. fertility rate. **In other words, Westoff and Wattenberg link the effects of abortion directly to fertility rates!**

It is also important to note that no real significant growth in the fertility rate occurs from 1973 to 1991, even though technology to enhance fertility and child bearing has improved in the past two decades (including for women over

35 years of age). Rather, women who are 35 and older that are finally having children after a delay, are contributing to the decline in the fertility rate. Wattenberg summarizes this phenomenom by stating, "Fertility delayed is fertility denied." (10)

The relationship between cumulative abortions and declining fertility rates are also reflected in Table 3.1.

**TABLE 3.1** - COMPARISON OF AGI AND CDC ABORTION STATISTICS AND TOTAL FERTILITY RATE. Note that the Total Fertility Rate includes women from 10-49 years and all races. The figures differ slightly from fertility rates in Graph 3.1 which focuses on women ages 15-44 for all races.

| Year | Annual Abortion Figures (AGI) | Cumulative Abortion Figures (AGI) | Cumulative Abortion Figures (CDC) | Total Fertil. Rate |
|------|------|------|------|------|
| 65 | | | | 2882 |
| 66 | | | | 2670 |
| 67 | | | | 2526 |
| 68 | | | | 2431 |
| 69 | | | | 2423 |
| 70 | | | 193,491 | 2480 |
| 71 | | | 679,307 | 2267 |
| 72 | | | 1,266,067 | 2010 |
| 73 | 744,610 | 744,610 | 1,881,898 | 1879 |
| 74 | 890,570 | 1,643,180 | 2,645,374 | 1835 |
| 75 | 1,034,170 | 2,677,350 | 3,500,227 | 1774 |
| 76 | 1,179,300 | 3,856,650 | 4,488,494 | 1738 |
| 77 | 1,316,700 | 5,173,350 | 5,567,924 | 1790 |
| 78 | 1,409,600 | 6,582,950 | 6,725,700 | 1760 |

| 79 | 1,497,570 | 8,080,520 | 7,977,621 | 1808 |
| 80 | 1,553,890 | 9,634,410 | 9,275,227 | 1840 |
| 81 | 1,577,340 | 11,211,750 | 10,575,987 | 1815 |
| 82 | 1,573,920 | 12,785,670 | 11,879,967 | 1829 |
| 83 | 1,575,000 | 14,360,670 | 13,148,954 | 1803 |
| 84 | 1,577,180 | 15,937,850 | 14,482,475 | 1805 |
| 85 | 1,588,550 | 17,526,400 | 15,811,475 | 1843 |
| 86 | 1,574,000 | 19,100,400 | 17,139,157 | 1836 |
| 87 | 1,559,110 | 20,659,510 | 18,492,828 | 1871 |
| 88 | 1,590,750 | 22,250,260 | 19,864,113 | 1932 |
| 89 | 1,566,900 | 23,817,160 | 21,260,771 | 2014 |
| 90 | 1,608,600 | 25,425,760 | 22,690,348 | 2090 |
| 91 | 1,556,500 | 26,982,260 | | 2075 |

Sources: AGI, CDC, National Center for Health Statistics

Note that the total fertility rate in Table 3.1 differs from the fertility rate in Graph 3.1. This discrepancy is due to the fact that the total fertility rate in table 3.1 measures women from 10 to 49 years of age, whereas the fertility rate in Graph 3.1 measures women from 15 to 44 years of age. Nevertheless, the total fertility rate drops from 1970 to 1972 and then an even sharper drop occurs starting at 1973 (the year Roe vs. Wade established abortion as a constitutional right). This total fertility rate decreased until 1988, when in 1989, it rose above the 1972 levels for the first time. Just, as the abortion numbers plateau with slow growth in the late 1970's and 1980's, so does the total fertility rate slowly rise. Note further that the 70-72 series as a contributing effect is supported when CDC abortion data is examined in Table 3.1 and compared with total fertility rates.

The total fertility rate statistics in Graph 3.1 and Table 3.1 differ from the more conventional fertility figures of 2.1

births per woman (for example). That system is expressed as lifetime births per woman. The fertility statistics listed in Graph 3.1 and Table 3.1 demonstrate a more sensitive method of describing yearly fertility rates and subtle shifts in those rates. It may be reassuring to note that the more common descriptor of total fertility rates agrees with the afore listed data. For a comparison, the total U.S. fertility rate from 1973-1989 has been below the critical population replacement level of 2.1 births per woman (averaging at about 1.8) (7,8,9).

Beside the individual effects of abortion on the general population fertility rate, the fertility rate of women that undergo abortions may be directed affected. A review by Huggins and Cullins examined abortion effects on fertility (11). Unfortunately, insufficient data exists concerning the effect of abortion on second pregnancies, spontaneous abortions, or low birth weight. However, the authors do state that abortion performed by poorly trained physicians or illegal abortions may result in infertility problems, especially due to infections. Earlier studies by Trichopoulos (12) stated that in Greece about 45 per cent of the cases of secondary infertility may be due to prior induced abortions. Studies by Hogue et al (13) and Daling and Emanuel (14) do not agree with this assertion. Former Surgeon General C. Everett Koop recommended in a report to President Reagan in 1987 that adverse effects by abortion on the mental and physical health of women require further study (15).

One infertility problem that is clearly appearing as a post-abortion complication is a condition known as Asherman's Syndrome. Asherman's Syndrome is the presence of intrauterine synechiae (i.e. tissue adhesions within the uterus) that produce clinical symptoms such as menstrual abnormalities, infertility, and habitual abortion (miscarriage)

(16). The incidence of Asherman's Syndrome, once thought to be low, is now recognized to be much greater in many countries. Furthermore, Klein and Garcia (16) note that with the legalization of abortion in the United States, that the incidence of Asherman's Syndrome will likely rise. Although the data is sparse, one indication of the rise of Asherman's Syndrome is hospital discharge surveys from The National Center of Health Statistics describing an increase from 1988 (7000 cases) to 1992 (9000 cases), with 1989 and 1991 each reporting 11,000 cases (41, 42, 43, 44, 45).

One of the main causes of Asherman's Syndrome is the surgical technique of dilatation and curettage (commonly referred to as a D&C), one of the most commonly used abortion techniques. The incidence of Asherman's Syndrome due to D&C becomes even more pronounced if a preexisting or post-operational infection occurs. Although Asherman's Syndrome can occur as a postoperative complication for a D&C that was not for an induced abortion, this text will focus on the consequences of legal induced abortion D&C procedures.

The diagnosis of Asherman's Syndrome is not always certain (16,17,18) Nevertheless, if the physician suspects Asherman's Syndrome, the best methods of detection are hysteroscopy (endoscopic examination of the uterus) and hysterosalpingography (X-ray examination of the uterus and the fallopian tubes following injection of a radio-opaque fluid) (16,17,18). The treatment usually involves cutting (lysing) the adhesions and subsequent treatment with estrogen and/or progesterone hormones and insertion of either an intrauterine device (IUD) or a Foley inflatable catheter (17, 18, 32). Following treatment of Asherman's Syndrome, the rate of fertility restoration is high, but not 100% (17).

If not treated, Asherman's Syndrome patients suffer with symptoms including infertility, menstrual irregularities, pelvic pain, miscarriages and ectopic pregnancy (16). Although the etiology (i.e. cause of the disease) behind how Asherman's Syndrome affects fertility is not totally certain, explanations include: the adhesions block sperm migration up in the uterus or that the embryo can not implant into the uterine lining, thus it implants in the cervix or fallopian tube (ectopic pregnancy) and/or a miscarriage occurs (16).

Unfortunately, studies by Shinagawa (33) and a more recent study by Dicker (34) indicate that either abortion, Asherman's Syndrome, or even the use of an IUD to treat Asherman's Syndrome will contribute to ectopic pregnancies. A unique (and formerly rare) form of ectopic pregnancy is cervical pregnancy. The incidence of cervical pregnancy reported in studies varies from 1 per 1,000 pregnancies to 1 per 18,000 pregnancies. Unfortunately, the numbers vary due in part to the fact that some cervical pregnancies go unnoticed and are recorded as spontaneous abortions (i.e. miscarriages) (34). Dicker (34) demonstrates evidence that the incidence of cervical pregnancy may be related to induced abortion, Asherman's Syndrome, or IUD treatment of Asherman's Syndrome. Note that the final treatment available for cervical pregnancies is usually a total hysterectomy (33,34). Thus, a long term complication of a D&C induced abortion may include Asherman's Syndrome leading to possible cervical pregnancy and finally a total hysterectomy.

Ismajovich et al (17) and March and Israel (18) report cases of Asherman's Syndrome appearing in women that have previously had legal induced abortions. It is important to note that D&C is one of the major surgical techniques used in legal abortions (19). Further long term studies may demonstrate an increase in the incidence of Asherman's Syndrome and cervical pregnancies, especially among women that have obtained abortions. Although the number of women having multiple abortions (and possibly multiple D&C procedures) is increasing (19), there are no studies that rule out multiple D&C procedures as another cause for Asherman's Syndrome. Finally, it must be noted that other factors can contribute to decreased fertility in women, including genetic defects and sexually transmitted disease-induced damage to reproductive organs.

Therefore, at least one possible complication for a woman who obtains an abortion (with D&C as the surgical method) is Asherman's Syndrome, which can result in infertility. This information must be added to the debate about abortion. Those obtaining an abortion should be informed about the possible complication of Asherman's Syndrome and its infertility effects.

Furthermore, women that have had abortions, especially those presently experiencing the above mentioned symptoms, may wish to be examined by their physician for Asherman's Syndrome. Recipients of an abortion should not suffer needlessly for actions done in the past.

In conclusion, the decline in total United States fertility rates coincides with the previously examined abortion data figures. Both the general fertility rate (for women ages 15-44) and the total fertility rate (for women ages 10-49) declined as abortion numbers increased throughout the 1970's and plateaued during the 1980's. This supports the earlier thesis that abortion is affecting the birth rate and the fertility rate (general and total) in the U.S. This decline in the fertility rate below replacement levels will eventually lead to a shrinking population in the U.S. (9). Consequences of a shrinking population will be discussed in later chapters.

Furthermore, evidence exists that abortion may directly affect the fertility of the recipient of an abortion. This may cause further long-term overall decline in the fertility rate in the United States.

# CHAPTER 4
# ADOPTION AND
# ABORTION-RELATED DEATHS

This chapter will explore two closely connected abortion consequences: the decrease in rates of adoption (the availability of unwanted births accepted by parents other than the biological parents) and the increase in abortion related deaths due to complications. Abortion related deaths were examined because legalization of abortion is reputed to decrease fatalities related to abortion complications (2,3).

## ADOPTION

The first topic, adoption, will be explored relative to the number of available children for adoption. As numbers of abortions increase, numbers of children available for adoptions decrease, instead of allowing children to come to term, they are terminated in large quantities.

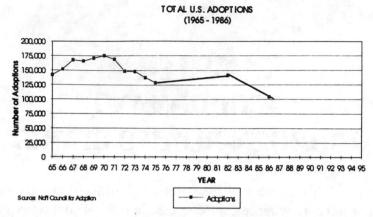

**GRAPH 4.1** - TOTAL U.S. ADOPTIONS FOR 1965-1986. Note: 1982 and 1986 figures based on surveys by the National Council for Adoption (20).

By examining Graph 4.1, notice that peak adoptions occurred in 1970. During this year, CDC records over 190,000 abortions (see Table 1.1). As numbers of abortions increased in the United Stated after 1970 (by both AGI and CDC data), the quanity of adoptions decreased. Note that after 1975, national recording of adoption stopped, but 1982 and 1986 studies support the premise that the numbers of U.S. adoptions declined (20). **This decline occurred while yearly U.S. abortions increased!**

## ABORTION RELATED DEATHS

Another interesting aspect of abortions, quanitities of abortion-related deaths, are reviewed in Graph 4.2.

ABORTION RELATED DEATHS IN U.S. (1972-1987)

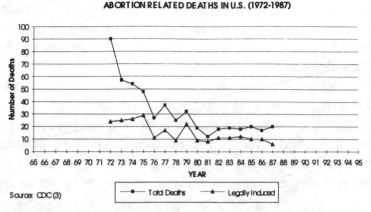

Source: CDC (3)    ■ Total Deaths    ▲ Legally Induced

**GRAPH 4.2** - COMPARISON OF TOTAL U.S. ABORTION-RELATED DEATHS AND LEGALLY-INDUCED ABORTION-RELATED DEATHS FOR 1972-1987. Note: total deaths includes abortion-related deaths categorized as legal induced, illegal induced, spontaneous, or unknown (3).

"Abortion-related death" is defined by a CDC study (3) as death resulting from; A) a direct complication of an abortion; B) an indirect complication caused by the chain of events initiated by the abortion; or C) aggravation of a preexisting condition by the physiologic or psychological effects of the abortion. The deaths were then categorized as "legal induced", "illegal induced", "spontaneous", or "unknown" (as to which type of abortion caused by death). Graph 4.2 focuses on legal induced abortion deaths and total abortion-related deaths.

While less than half of the total abortion deaths were due to legal induced abortions in 1970 (20 deaths by legal induced abortions versus a total of 90 deaths), legal induced abortions accounted for between 30 to over 60 percent of the abortion related deaths during the 1980's. The risk of death still occurs even after 20 years of improvements in medical technology and after the legalization of abortion to end "backalley botched" abortions.

One study by Atrash et al (21) stated that the leading causes of death as a result of legal abortion during the 1979-1985 period, were anesthesia; followed by hemorrhage, embolism, and infection, respectively. The risk of legal abortion-induced deaths was also higher among older women, among black or other races, and among those obtaining abortion at a later gestational age (i.e. 16 weeks or later).

One other factor that may contribute to abortion related deaths is described in two studies by Henshaw and Van Vort (5,39) and is seen in Graph 4.3.

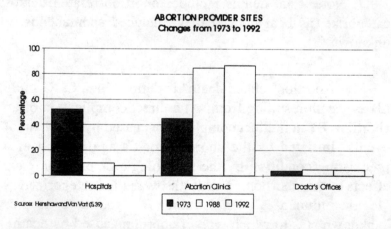

GRAPH 4.3 - COMPARISON OF ABORTION PROVIDER SITES FOR 1973-1992.

The authors of that study note that the distribution of abortion providers (i.e. facilities that perform abortions) shifted substantially from hopsitals to clinics. In 1973, the distribution of providers was as follows: hospitals, about 51%; clinics 46%; and doctors offices about 3%. This had changed dramatically by 1988, when the distribution of abortion providers was: clinics 86%, hospitals 10%, and doctors offices about 4%. By 1992, the proportional distribution had changed further to: clinics 89%, hospitals 7%, and doctors offices 4%.

The authors noted that hospital services are needed for women with health conditions that could lead to complications (including death). These services include equipment to deal with blood transfusion, cardiac arrest, uterine puncture, etc. Furthermore, this issue has become so important that the authors note that, by 1992, some abortion providers required hospital facilities for their high risk patients (39). PERHAPS the decline in the availability of hospital services could be a factor in some abortion related fatalities.

Although CDC (3) lists the case fatality rate (i.e. the rate of deaths due to legal induced abortions per 100,000) at 0.4 percent in 1987 (latest count), it should be stressed that death is still a possible complication for abortion patients. WOMEN WHO UNDERGO ABORTION PROCEDURES MUST BE REMINDED THAT DEATH IS STILL A REAL POSSIBILITY FOR THIS PROCEDURE!

In conclusion, the data strongly demonstrate that abortion has affected the adoption rate. This is likely because of a reduced pool of adoptable children due to the termination of unwanted pregnancies.

The risk of abortion related death, while declining since the 1970's, still exists. The major factors in abortion-related deaths include the use of anesthesia, more advanced age of the women, race, and the higher gestational age of the fetus at time of abortion. Although medical technology has made significant improvements since the 1970's, death remains a small, but real possibility for abortion patients.

# CHAPTER 5
# UNMASKING ABORTION
# EFFECTS ON POPULATION
# GROWTH

## BASIC POPULATION DATA

This chapter examines the effect of abortion on United States population growth. It attempts to remove factors that might mask statistically significant abortion effects. It also examines U.S. population growth projections IF abortions had not occurred.

Measuring United States population growth is not merely a matter of counting the number of people present in the U.S. In order to look at real population growth of the indigenous population (i.e. growth of the presently residing population), then you need to remove extraneous numbers. The most significant extraneous effect on population growth is immigration. U.S. emigration effects are believed to be remote since U.S. emigration is estimated to be only about 100,000 per year (6).

Merely removing the yearly immigration statistics from the total population statistics does not ensure accuracy. Rather, since immigration has a cumulative effect on population growth, the cumulative effect of immigration needs to be subtracted from the total population numbers. This results in

31

an adjusted U.S. population number which more accurately reflects indigenous population numbers and can indicate real population growth. In short, removing the additive effect of immigration will help determine real population growth. This is demonstrated by Table 5.1.

REMEMBER, one good way to fully understand a table of data is to use a ruler or straightedge and follow down the page horizontal to each row of data (start at the year 1965 and lay the ruler across all of the numbered columns).

**TABLE 5.1**-EXAMINATION OF THE U.S. POPULATION FIGURES COMPARING THE EFFECTS OF IMMIGRATION (YEARLY AND CUMULATIVE). Adjusted U.S. population figures developed by subtracting cumulative immigration figures from Bureau of Census population data. Cumulative immigration defined as the summation of yearly immigration figures (start year for this exercise, 1965).

| Year | U.S. Population Figures | Yearly Immigration Figures | Cumulative Immigration Figures | Adjusted U.S. Population Figures |
|---|---|---|---|---|
| 65 | 194,303,000 | 296,697 | 296,697 | 193,683,263 |
| 66 | 196,560,000 | 323,040 | 619,737 | 195,940,263 |
| 67 | 198,712,000 | 361,972 | 981,709 | 197,730,291 |
| 68 | 200,706,000 | 454,448 | 1,436,157 | 199,269,843 |
| 69 | 202,677,000 | 358,579 | 1,794,736 | 200,882,264 |
| 70 | 205,052,000 | 373,326 | 2,168,062 | 202,883,938 |
| 71 | 207,661,000 | 370,478 | 2,538,540 | 205,122,460 |
| 72 | 209,896,000 | 384,685 | 2,923,225 | 206,972,775 |
| 73 | 211,909,000 | 400,063 | 3,323,288 | 208,585,712 |
| 74 | 213,854,000 | 394,861 | 3,718,149 | 210,135,851 |

| | | | | |
|---|---|---|---|---|
| 75 | 215,973,000 | 386,194 | 4,104,343 | 211,868,657 |
| 76 | 218,035,000 | 398,613 | 4,502,956 | 213,532,044 |
| 77 | 220,239,000 | 462,315 | 4,965,271 | 215,273,729 |
| 78 | 222,585,000 | 601,442 | 5,566,713 | 217,018,287 |
| 79 | 225,055,000 | 460,348 | 6,027,061 | 219,027,939 |
| 80 | 227,722,000 | 530,639 | 6,557,700 | 221,164,300 |
| 81 | 229,958,000 | 596,600 | 7,154,300 | 222,803,700 |
| 82 | 232,192,000 | 594,131 | 7,748,431 | 224,443,569 |
| 83 | 234,321,000 | 559,763 | 8,308,194 | 226,012,806 |
| 84 | 236,370,000 | 543,903 | 8,852,097 | 227,517,903 |
| 85 | 238,492,000 | 570,009 | 9,422,106 | 229,069,894 |
| 86 | 240,680,000 | 601,708 | 10,023,814 | 230,656,186 |
| 87 | 242,836,000 | 601,516 | 10,625,330 | 232,210,670 |
| 88 | 245,057,000 | 643,025 | 11,268,355 | 233,788,645 |
| 89 | 247,343,000 | 1.090.924 | 12,359,279 | 234,983,721 |
| 90 | 249,942,000 | 1,536,483 | 13,893,762 | 236,028,238 |
| 91 | 252,688,000 | 1,827,167 | 15,722,929 | 236,965,071 |

Source: Bureau of Census, Immigration and Naturalization Service (INS)

Note the major differences between yearly U.S. population and the Adjusted U.S. Population when the cumulative effects of immigration (especially in the 1980's and 1990's) are removed. It has been stated that the U.S. population growth has been assisted by immigration. Westoff (6) states that if it were not for immigration (under the present low fertility rate), the U.S. would stop growing and begin to see a decline in population by the middle of the next century.

Furthermore, it has been suggested that the U.S. should INCREASE its level of legal immigration to fill the gap in its falling birth rate and the subsequent slowing of population growth (22). Westoff (6) states that perhaps the next population commission (i.e. The Commission on Population

33

Growth and the American Future, which meets periodically to examine U.S. population growth and its consequences to the nation) will be pondering ways to induce marriage and childbearing in the U.S.

Also, note that the 1989 to 1991 period experienced an increase in immigration numbers, but this was not necessarily from recent arrivals into the U.S. Rather, this statistical increase in legal immigration was actually only on paper and reflected an acknowledgement of immigrants already in the country, pursant to the immigration amnesty program set up in 1987. This program granted amnesty to illegal immigrants in the county and allowed them to become legal immigrants during the registration years of 1989 to 1991, substantially skewing the statistics. These immigrants had to have entered the U.S. illegally prior to 1982. The Bureau of Census states that the illegal immigration may be several times higher than the legal number of immigrants in the U.S. (23)

When the cumulative immigration statistics are compared to the cumulative effect of abortion (see GRAPH 5.1), several aspects can be noted.

First, note that immigration does NOT replace the numbers of aborted lives. Therefore, a net decrease in growth still exists even after immigration numbers are inserted in an attempt to replace the aborted births. Furthermore, note that the immigration curve slopes upward during the immigration amnesty period of 1989-1991. Even with this enhanced legal registration of immigrants, the immigrant numbers do not replace the losses (in population growth) due to abortion.

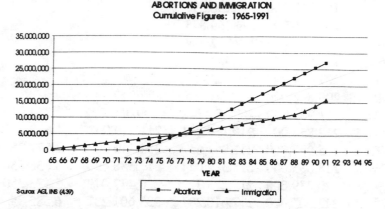

ABORTIONS AND IMMIGRATION
Cumulative Figures: 1965-1991

**GRAPH 5.1** - COMPARSION OF CUMULATIVE U.S. ABORTIONS AND CUMULATIVE U.S. IMMIGRATION FOR 1965-1991.

## ABORTION EFFECTS ON POPULATION GROWTH

The effects of abortion on population growth can be more accurately described by Table 5.2.

**TABLE 5.2**-COMPARISON OF U.S. POPULATION DATA AND THE CUMULATIVE EFFECTS OF ABORTION. Adjusted U.S. population figures developed as explained in Table 5.1.

| Year | U.S. Population Figures | Adjusted U.S. Population Figures | Adjusted U.S. Population Plus Cumul. Abortions | Cumulative Abortions |
|------|------------------------|----------------------------------|-----------------------------------------------|---------------------|
| 65 | 194,303,000 | 193,683,263 | | |

35

| | | | |
|---|---|---|---|
| 66 | 196,560,000 | 195,940,263 | | |
| 67 | 198,712,000 | 197,730,291 | | |
| 68 | 200,706,000 | 199,269,843 | | |
| 69 | 202,677,000 | 200,882,264 | | |
| 70 | 205,052,000 | 202,883,938 | | |
| 71 | 207,661,000 | 205,122,460 | | |
| 72 | 209,896,000 | 206,972,775 | | |
| 73 | 211,909,000 | 208,585,712 | 209,330,322 | 744,610 |
| 74 | 213,854,000 | 210,135,851 | 211,779,031 | 1,643,180 |
| 75 | 215,973,000 | 211,868,657 | 214,546,007 | 2,677,350 |
| 76 | 218,035,000 | 213,532,044 | 217,388,694 | 3,856,650 |
| 77 | 220,239,000 | 215,273,729 | 220,447,079 | 5,173,350 |
| 78 | 222,585,000 | 217,018,287 | 223,601,237 | 6,582,950 |
| 79 | 225,055,000 | 219,027,939 | 227,108,459 | 8,080,520 |
| 80 | 227,722,000 | 221,164,300 | 230,798,710 | 9,634,410 |
| 81 | 229,958,000 | 222,803,700 | 234,015,450 | 11,211,750 |
| 82 | 232,192,000 | 224,443,569 | 237,229,239 | 12,785,670 |
| 83 | 234,321,000 | 226,012,806 | 240,373,476 | 14,360,670 |
| 84 | 236,370,000 | 227,517,903 | 243,455,753 | 15,937,850 |
| 85 | 238,492,000 | 229,069,894 | 246,596,294 | 17,526,400 |
| 86 | 240,680,000 | 230,656,186 | 249,756,586 | 19,100,400 |
| 87 | 242,836,000 | 232,210,670 | 252,870,180 | 20,659,510 |
| 88 | 245,057,000 | 233,788,645 | 256,038,905 | 22,250,260 |
| 89 | 247,343,000 | 234,983,721 | 258,800,881 | 23,817,160 |
| 90 | 249,942,000 | 236,028,238 | 261,453,998 | 25,425,760 |
| 91 | 252,688,000 | 236,965,071 | 263,947,331 | 26,982,260 |

Source: AGI, INS, Bureau of Census

With the U.S. population adjusted for cumulative abortion effects, an added set of figures can be compared with earlier figures in Table 5.1. NOTICE that as of 1973, the abortion figures were added to adjusted U.S. population figures. By 1991, note the differences between U.S. Bureau of Census population figures, adjusted U.S. population figures (remember; figures WITHOUT immigration effects), and finally the U.S. adjusted population figure WITH cumulative abortion numbers added. These figures suggest that U.S. population growth would have been significantly higher, IF abortions were not performed. This data supports the earlier statement that immigration is not replacing the lost numbers due to abortion.

Another way to examine population growth is to examine the percentage of yearly change in the population. To further examine the effects of abortion, the adjusted U.S. population figures were examined with and without the abortion numbers. This might help indicate whether abortion numbers would have noticably contributed to yearly (adjusted) population growth (see Graph 5.2).

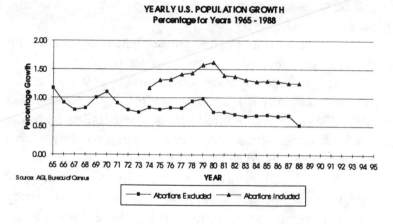

**GRAPH 5.2** - COMPARISON OF CHANGE IN YEARLY U.S. POPULATION GROWTH WITH AND WITHOUT YEARLY ABORTION FIGURES ADDED. Note: U.S. population figures are the "adjusted" figures as described in Table 5.1. Each point reflects percentage growth as compared with data from prior year.

37

It is important to note when the decline in U.S. population growth occurred; at the beginning of the 1970's, just when the legalization of abortion came into effect in the United States. The last peak of U.S. population growth occurred in 1971, at the time when legal abortions were increasing (based on CDC data, see Table 3.1). Note that the percentage of U.S. population growth would have been higher with the cumulative abortion numbers added. Also, note that if the 70-72 series had been added, it would have turned the percentage population growth upward. Another important point to notice is the general flattening of growth (plateau) below the 1.0% mark from 1971 forward while, with the abortion numbers, the U.S. population growth exceeds 1.0% from 1973-1988. This is important, as population growth (as it will be shown in later sections) is important for economic growth.

A clear example of the consequences of a declining population growth, and perhaps a portent of what is in store for the United States by the early to middle 21st Century, is Italy. Predominantly Roman Catholic Italy legalized abortion in 1978 (35). Recent United Nations and Italian National Statistics Institute studies have determined that Italy's birth rate is the lowest in all of Europe (36,37).

At 1.21 childbirths per woman, this rate is very low indeed, when compared to a birthrate of 2.1, which is necessary to sustain a country's population level. In 1993, for example, 5,265 MORE Italians died than were born (37). At this present rate, within 100 years, the population of 57 million will shrink to 15 million with half of the population over 60 years of age. Even if the Italian birthrate rose overnight to 2.0, it would still take 30 years for the population to grow (46). In essence, Italy's population is shrinking as well as greying. Therefore, while the older segment of Italy's population is expanding, this will increase the retirement tax (e.g. Social Security, etc.) burden on the shrinking younger segment of the population.

If this trend persists, it will have serious consequences on a number of economic, military, and social variables like national security, economic growth, tax revenues, etc. Even now, Italian cities like Venice, are actively competing for the sparse number of students to maintain teaching jobs in their schools (46). Although other factors may play a role in Italy's declining birth rate (e.g. working women, economics, delaying marriage, etc. (36,37), abortion, as previously stated Westoff (6) and Wattenberg (9) plays a serious role in the decling birth rate of a nation (and perhaps the subsequent decline of the nation as a whole!). Italy may be the first modern day case of a nation in decline with abortion as a contributing factor.

In conclusion, the data indicates that legal induced abortions have affected U.S. population growth significantly. Legal abortions have affected the total U.S. population numbers AND the percentage of yearly growth. Furthermore, as the number of yearly abortions increased, the United States. population growth continued to decrease. The decrease in growth percentage may not be due merely to increasing numbers of abortions but may also be due to the cumulative effect of abortions.

The cumulative effect of abortions would be especially apparent when you consider that those aborted in the early 1970's would be of reproductive age in the late 1980's and early 1990's. Wattenberg refers to these effects in which reduced births in the first generation leading to further reductions in births in the second generation as "the birth dearth" (24). This term first coined by Wattenberg in 1971, also refers to when the total fertility rate drops below the "replacement level" of 2.1 children per woman. As this chapter and chapter 3 have demonstrated, both of these factors exist in the United States today. Further economic and social effects of this phenomena will be demonstrated in subsequent chapters.

# CHAPTER 6
# ABORTION EFFECTS ON EDUCATION
# STUDENT ENROLLMENT AND TEACHER EMPLOYMENT

One of the first social arenas affected by abortion is education. This is because one of the first social institutions that the aborted child would have entered is the educational system (Other social institutions include the church, the military, the employment sector, college, the family, etc.). Therefore, the abortion removes a consumer of educational services (e.g. teacher services) and goods (e.g. books, paper supplies, etc.) at the primary, secondary, and higher education levels. This work focuses on abortion effects at the primary (Kindergarten to 8th grade) and at the secondary (9th to 12th grade) education levels. The primary source for the education statistics is the United States Department of Education (DOE). As abortion effects are currently less than 30 years in length, future studies may demonstrate abortion effects in higher education as well as another institution that young adults enter at the age range 17-22, the military (see Chapter 10).

Let's look first at the relationship between student enrollment and abortion (see Graph 6.1).

THE COST OF ABORTION

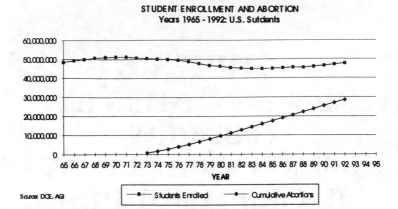

STUDENT ENROLLMENT AND ABORTION
Years 1965 - 1992: U.S. Students

**GRAPH 6.1** - COMPARISON OF YEARLY U.S. STUDENT ENROLLMENT WITH CUMULATIVE U.S. ABORTIONS FOR 1965-1990. Note: U.S. student enrollment includes total public and private school student enrollment (for grades kindergarten through 12th grade). Student enrollment is cited for the fall of the listed year.

To detect the effects of abortion on education, we must first note that a five year lag exists from time of birth and entry into kindergarten. Notice that the student enrollment decreases from the mid-1970's and continues through out the 1980's. A clear depression exists by 1978 (five years after legal abortions existed through out the U.S.), but the decline existed earlier. This may be due to the 70-72 series. This point is futher supported when you notice that, after years of slow decline, the drop in student enrollment accelerates during the period of 1980-1984 coincides with the time that the yearly abortion rate exceeds 1 million during the period of 1975-

1979 (see Table 1.1, Graph 1.1, Table 6.1, and Graph 6.1). **As abortions were legalized nationally in 1973, student enrollment began to fall significantly!**

Note also that as the cumulative abortion figures increase, the slope of student enrollment (e.g. student growth) flattens out. This suggests a cumulative effect from abortions. In other words, as the aggregate number of abortions increases, the loss of students becomes more clearly seen in the enrollment figures (and in the job opportunities in education-but more on that later!).

As mentioned earlier, abortions' effects on education is delayed five years (from birth to kindergarten) before changes in school numbers can be observed. The following table (see Table 6.1) was developed to demonstrate the "missing students effect" from kindergarten to 12th grade for each abortion year (based on AGI data). For example, 1991 would have 18,355,790 more students when the sum of abortions between 1974 to 1986 are added (adjusted for five years delay until entry into kindergarten). This series of figures is important, and are used in further calculations through the rest of the chapter. The total U.S. enrolled student figures are added for reference.

**TABLE 6.1**-ANALYSIS OF "MISSING STUDENTS" VIA ABORTION THROUGH THE SCHOOL ENTRY YEARS KINDERGARTEN THROUGH 12TH GRADE (AGES 5 TO 18 INCLUSIVELY). Note that total U.S. student enrolled for those years are given for reference. Total student enrollment year is measured at fall of the year listed.

43

# THE COST OF ABORTION

| Year | Abortions resulting in "Missing Students" | Total of U.S. Students Enrolled |
|------|-------------------------------------------|--------------------------------|
| 78 | 744,610 | 47,637,000 |
| 79 | 1,635,180 | 46,651,000 |
| 80 | 2,677,350 | 46,208,000 |
| 81 | 3,856,650 | 45,544,000 |
| 82 | 5,173,350 | 45,166,000 |
| 83 | 6,582,950 | 44,967,000 |
| 84 | 8,080,520 | 44,908,000 |
| 85 | 9,634,410 | 44,979,000 |
| 86 | 11,211,750 | 45,205,000 |
| 87 | 12,785,670 | 45,205,000 |
| 88 | 14,360,670 | 45,430,000 |
| 89 | 15,937,850 | 45,898,000 |
| 90 | 17,526,400 | 46,450,000 |
| 91 | 18,355,790 | |
| 92 | 19,016,330 | |
| 93 | 19,572,910 | |
| 94 | 19,960,510 | |
| 95 | 20,252,410 | |

Source: AGI, Department of Education (DOE)


Another way to demonstrate the effect on abortion on student enrollment is described in Graph 6.2. The graph answers the question; what would have student enrollment been IF the total student enrollment included the abortion numbers?

# ABORTION EFFECTS ON EDUCATION

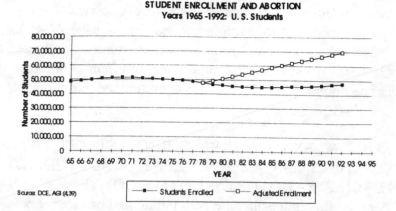

STUDENT ENROLLMENT AND ABORTION
Years 1965 -1992: U. S. Students

Source: DOE, AGI (4,37)

**GRAPH 6.2** - COMPARISON OF YEARLY U.S. STUDENT ENROLLMENT WITH AND WITHOUT YEARLY U.S. ABORTION FIGURES. Note: adjusted student enrollment figures based on U.S. student enrollment added to "missing student effect" figures (see Table 6.1) for that respective year. Total student enrollment is cited for the fall of the listed year.

This enrollment curve describes the enrollment with and without the abortion figures. The abortion figures are based on the cumulative numbers from the "missing student effect" as described in Table 6.1. For example, those aborted in 1973 would have entered kindergarten in 1978, and therefore these numbers are added as "adjusted enrollment" in 1978 figures. Note the increases in the adjusted student enrollment curve, especially as the cumulative effect of abortion becomes more apparent in the 1980's. The final numbers in 1990 describe the total number of students enrolled in the United States at 46,450,000. Yet, with the aborted lives, the adjusted student enrollment in that year would have been 63,976,400!

45

This last point suggests serious consequences beyond mere student enrollment statistics. The economic effects on new school construction, computer purchases, sales of books and school supplies, etc., are all affected by student enrollment numbers. Another social (and economic) effect of abortion can be demonstrated by the effects on teacher employment (see TABLE 6.2).

**TABLE 6.2**-EXAMINATION OF UNITED STATES TOTAL TEACHERS, ENROLLED STUDENTS, AND STUDENT/TEACHER RATIO FOR FALL OF SCHOOL YEARS 1965-1991. Note: Figures include both public and private schools and cover from kindergarten to 12th grade. 1991 figures are estimated. Total student enrollment is cited for fall of listed year.

| Year | Student Teacher Ratio | Total Number of U.S. Teachers | Total of U.S. Students Enrolled |
|---|---|---|---|
| 65 | 25.10 | 1,933,000 | 48,368,000 |
| 66 | 24.50 | 2,012,000 | 49,242,000 |
| 67 | 24.00 | 2,079,000 | 49,890,000 |
| 68 | 23.50 | 2,161,000 | 50,703,000 |
| 69 | 22.70 | 2,245,000 | 51,050,000 |
| 70 | 22.40 | 2,292,000 | 51,257,000 |
| 71 | 22.40 | 2,293,000 | 51,271,000 |
| 72 | 21.70 | 2,337,000 | 50,445,000 |
| 73 | 21.30 | 2,372,000 | 50,445,000 |
| 74 | 20.80 | 2,410,000 | 50,073,000 |
| 75 | 20.30 | 2,453,000 | 49,819,000 |
| 76 | 20.10 | 2,457,000 | 49,478,000 |
| 77 | 19.60 | 2,488,000 | 48,717,000 |

| | | | |
|---|---|---|---|
| 78 | 19.20 | 2,479,000 | 47,637,000 |
| 79 | 19.00 | 2,461,000 | 46,651,000 |
| 80 | 18.60 | 2,486,000 | 46,208,000 |
| 81 | 18.70 | 2,440,000 | 45,544,000 |
| 82 | 18.40 | 2,458,000 | 45,166,000 |
| 83 | 18.20 | 2,476,000 | 44,967,000 |
| 84 | 17.90 | 2,508,000 | 44,908,000 |
| 85 | 17.60 | 2,549,000 | 44,979,000 |
| 86 | 17.40 | 2,592,000 | 45,205,000 |
| 87 | 17.30 | 2,632,000 | 45,205,000 |
| 88 | 17.00 | 2,668,000 | 45,430,000 |
| 89 | 16.80 | 2,734,000 | 45,898,000 |
| 90 | 16.90 | 2,751,000 | 46,450,000 |
| 91 | 16.90 | 2,786,000 | 47,032,000 |

Source: Department of Education

Table 6.2 describes student/teacher ratios for the years 1965-1991. Note the nearly 1.1 million drop in students during the fall of 1978 (as compared to 1977 figures). This is also the year that the 1973 aborted numbers would have entered school in kindergarten (the first sign of the "missing student effect").

As time progresses, the student teacher ratio declines. One explanation for this phenomenon could be that student enrollment declined while the teacher population remained stable. This argument is nullified upon closer examination of the number of U.S. teachers in Table 6.2. Despite the decline in student enrollment, the number of U.S. teachers increased. Furthermore, while the total number of U.S. teachers increased from 1965 to 1990, the total number of U.S. students decreased. Remember, that while teacher positions increased and student enrollment decreased, abortions (both yearly AND cumulative) continued to increase in the 1970's and 1980's (see Graph 1.1 and 1.2).

If all the aborted lives were calculated as enrolled students (see Graph 6.2), the resultant teaching positions lost due to abortion could be calculated. Using 1973 and 1990 teacher/student ratios (1973-for the year of Roe vs. Wade and 1990-for the most recent ratio available) and the "missing student effect" figures from Table 6.1, the teacher job losses due to abortion are described (see Graph 6.3).

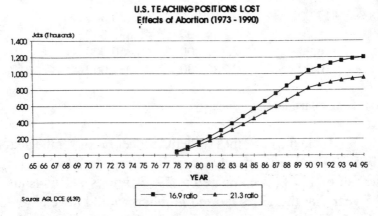

**GRAPH 6.3** - COMPARISON OF U.S. TEACHING POSITIONS LOST TO ABORTION USING "MISSING STUDENT EFFECT" FIGURES AND STUDENT/ TEACHER RATIOS FOR 1973 (21.3) AND 1990 (16.9) Note: methodology for attaining "missing student effect" explained in Table 6.1.

Notice that in fall of 1995, the cumulative aborted lives that would have entered school in kindergarten through 12th grade (the sum of abortion figures for years 1978 to 1990; see Table 6.1), would have meant the creation of between

950,000 to 1.2 million more teaching positions! **Clearly, one cost of abortion is teacher jobs!**

Furthermore, due to later increases in abortion numbers in the late 1970's and 1980's (see Graph 1.1), these numbers of lost teaching positions will continue to increase throughout the 1990's. The cumulative effect of abortions will continue to be felt throughout the 1990's in both student enrollment and in teacher employment opportunities.

In conclusion, the evidence suggests that the social and economic effects of abortion on education include declining student enrollment, reduced available teaching positions, reduced economic growth of school related materials (e.g. computers, books, paper, desks, etc.) and, fewer education construction requirements (e.g. construction of new schools, expansion of present education facilities, etc.).

Sadly, the National Education Association (NEA) of the United States supports abortion (25), even recently reaffirming support for abortion rights in its 1993-94 NEA convention resolutions. That is like the United Auto Workers union voting to support the banning of the automobile! I question whether teachers (especially unemployed teachers) realize that their union endorses policies that reduce their job opportunities.

It should also be noted that the NEA is not the only labor union to support abortion. The State, County & Municipal Employees and The Service Employees International have passed pro-abortion resolutions, while even the formidable AFL-CIO is contending with pro-abortion sentiments (26).

49

# CHAPTER 7
# ABORTION EFFECTS ON ECONOMIC GROWTH (GROSS DOMESTIC PRODUCT)

This chapter will examine evidence that abortion has had an effect on United States economic growth. Although this author does not claim that these problems are purely the result of abortion, closer examination of select economic indicators (as Chapters 7, 8, and 9 will explore) may reveal that abortion contributes to U.S. economic problems.

For this chapter, I used data from the U.S. Bureau of Economic Analysis. But, If you wish to examine only U.S. DOMESTIC (i.e. within the 50 American states) production of goods and services, you need to use the economic statistical measure known as the Gross Domestic Product (GDP). A question arises: Why not instead Gross National Product (GNP) data?

Simply put, GDP measures the total productivity of goods and services in the United States regardless if produced by U.S. owned companies or foreign owned companies. The GNP covers goods and services produced by U.S. companies both within the U.S. and abroad, but not production by foreign owned companies. For instance, GNP measures Ford Motor productivity of Ford plants in Detroit and Denmark, but not of the Toyota plant in Kentucky. BUT, GDP measures productivity of a Ford plant ONLY in Detroit, not Denmark, and it will measure productivity of the Toyota plant in Kentucky (but not in Tokyo). The attempt to measure U.S. productivity (goods and services) and compare it to "possible workers and consumers" (i.e. aborted lives) will give a better comparison of the effects of abortion on U.S. productivity and consumption with the GDP figures.

Graph 7.1 compares the U.S. Gross Domestic Product (GDP) and the cumulative effect of abortion. The yearly percentile change of GDP was used as the measure of change (i.e. growth). The yearly percentile change measurement of GDP can be sensitive to smaller variations, whereas decade comparative studies might not be so revealing (e.g. compare GDP growth for 1970-1980). This is especially helpful when one measures the cumulative effect of abortions. As the cumulative number of abortions (i.e. missing consumers and producers of goods and services) goes up, the yearly impact on the economy will increase. Therefore, over time, the cumulative effect of abortion should increase and become easier to detect on yearly economic growth measurements.

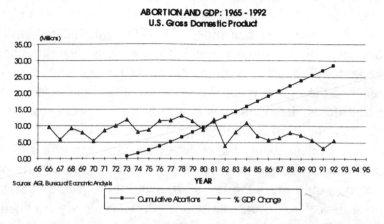

**GRAPH 7.1** - COMPARISON OF CUMULATIVE ABORTION EFFECTS AND U.S. GROSS DOMESTIC PRODUCT (GDP) FROM 1965-1992. Note that the yearly GDP percentage change was developed by comparison of that year's GDP figures with the prior year's figures and then developed into a percentile. Percentage change figures based on GDP figures in current (1993) dollars.

Upon review of Graph 7.1, as the cumulative effect of abortion rises, especially in the 1980's, the slope of GDP growth continues to decline, from the late 1970's forward. This suggests that real GDP growth continued to slow down as the cumulative effect of abortion becomes more apparent. It is interesting to note that the slide in GDP continued during the era of Reaganomics in the 1980's, a time normally associated with growth and prosperity. Granted, tax cuts may have spurred economic growth, but the reductions in consumers and the early effects of reductions in the labor force due to abortions could explain in part the effects of GDP

53

decline. The cumulative effect caused by abortions will continue to persist even though some GDP growth will exist. GDP growth will continue, but will continue to spiral downward as the cumulative effect of abortions becomes more apparent. When many of these aborted lives would have reached the age to enter the work force and purchase "big ticket items" like cars, new homes, vacation packages, etc., their absence will be increasingly felt in the statistics.

In conclusion, the effect of abortion can affect U.S. domestic economic activity. As the cumulative effects of abortion built up in the late 1970's and through the 1980's, regardless of U.S. economic policies, the GDP slowly declined. Remember, even though the percentage of GDP wiggled up and down, the eventual result was a slow downward trend. The explanation for this (putting aside smaller factors which cause year to year changes) relationship between rising cumulative abortion figures and downward percentage of GDP change is that economic growth slowed as the number of consumers (and later producers) decline. The aborted lives resulted in fewer consumers (e.g. diapers, toys, food, school books, clothes) and fewer producers (e.g. summer workers, cheap part time labor, etc.)

Eventually, these effects will be felt in other economic sectors, especially "big ticket" items like cars and housing.

# CHAPTER 8
# ABORTION AND
# PERSONAL INCOME

The effect of abortion on economic growth as seen in Chapter 7 can be reinforced by examining the relationship between abortion and personal income (see Graph 8.1). Remember, these studies focus on percentage of income change. We will examine if a trend or relationship exists between cumulative abortions and the overall direction (not merely a yearly measure) of percentage income change.

Notice the similarity of the decline of growth in personal income curve as compared to the decline in the GDP percentile curve. As the cumulative abortions increased from the late 1970's through the 1980's (again despite the Reagan era of economic growth), the percentage of personal income change progressed in a downward trend. As the 1980's progressed, economic growth occurs, but it was gradually declining overall, even into the 1990's.

There are many small and large factors that can affect the economic data (e.g. inflation, changing government policies, trade deficits, weather), but these factors do not necessarily affect the overall direction of growth or change. Population growth shifts CAN affect economic factors, both yearly and in the overall direction of growth. One method of inducing a population growth shift is abortion. Fewer births

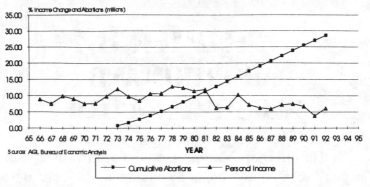

**GRAPH 8.1** - COMPARISON OF CUMULATIVE ABORTIONS AND PERSONAL INCOME AS A PERCENTAGE OF CHANGE. Note that the method developed to determine the percentage of change of personal income is similar to Graph 7.1. Percentage change figures based on personal income figures in current (1993) dollars.

mean fewer laborers to produce goods and services. Fewer births also mean less consumption of goods and services. With a decrease of laborers and consumers, the eventual result is a decrease in economic activity.

As economic activity declines, personal income growth (as with GDP) eventually declines. The overall decline in the personal income is directly affected by cumulative abortions. As the number of cumulative abortions increase, the decline in the economic growth patterns (i.e. personal income and GDP) will become more apparent. Furthermore, the economic activity declines (especially in personal income) will become enhanced as those early aborted lives would have entered higher income positions.

56

In conclusion, the evidence suggests that as cumulative abortions have increased, the GDP and personal income have declined. Although other factors may have also played a role in these declines, abortion contributes to diminishing consumption of goods and services, as well as reducing the available labor pool in the U.S. market place. Although these results are preliminary since most of the aborted lives would be entering the job market at the lower wage scale in the late 1980's and 1990's, these effects will become more apparent in later years when those lives would have been entering the middle to higher incomes brackets (perhaps by 1995 to 2020).

# CHAPTER 9
## ABORTION AND TAXATION
## (FEDERAL REVENUES)

This chapter examines the effect of abortion on taxation. The premise for this investigation is that aborted lives would have contributed to federal revenues via labor performed, resulting in payment of income taxes and social security, as well as by paying taxes on goods and services consumed. Due to variations in state taxation policies, I have focused on federal revenues only.

Recent attention has focused on the U.S. public deficit and public debt (see Graph 9.1 and 9.2). Remember, it is the yearly federal budget deficit that accrues into a cumulative long-term U.S. public debt. Although these problems are certainly not purely the result of abortion, closer examination of select economic indicators reveals that abortion may contribute to these problems.

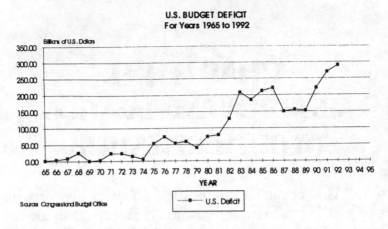

**GRAPH 9.1** - YEARLY U.S. BUDGET DEFICIT FOR 1965-1992.

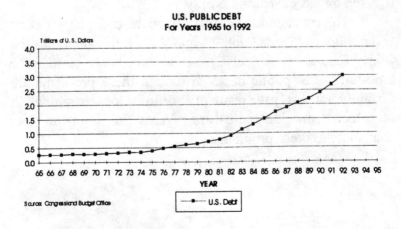

**GRAPH 9.2** - CUMULATIVE U.S. BUDGET DEBT FOR 1965-1992.

As these debt-factors (national deficit and debt) illustrated in graph 9.1 and 9.2 increase over time, it would be useful to examine the amount of potential tax revenue that would have been generated if the aborted lives would have arrived at income producing age. It must be stressed that these figures are preliminary, as the true effects may not be completely understood until well beyond 2000. It must be acknowledged that prior to age 17, the income (and therefore tax revenue generation) of most of the aborted lives would have been small. BUT, as each aborted life passed age 17, most would have produced income, and consumption of goods and services and therefore tax revenues would accrue to the U.S. Treasury.

To simplify this estimate, I have selected to take the cumulative abortion numbers (AGI figures for 1991) and estimate federal tax revenues based on Internal Revenue Service (IRS) data for 1991 (see TABLE 9.1).

**TABLE 9.1**-ESTIMATED TOTAL FEDERAL TAX REVENUES COLLECTED BY CUMULATIVE ABORTED LIVES FOR 1991. NOTE: calculation was based on most recent data available (1991 for abortion data, 1991 for tax data).

$5006.00$_a$ x 26,982,260$_b$ = $\underline{\$135,073,193,560.00}$ Federal tax revenues collected

a-average total tax liability for 1991 (27).
b-total cumulative abortions from 1973-1991 (4,39).

Granted, this takes into consideration that all members of the aborted lives are employable, and would be employed full time at the time of tax collection. **It should be noted that the above "missing tax revenue" was ONE HALF (50.1% of the 269.50 billion dollar deficit) of the U.S. budget deficit for 1991** (see Graph 9.1). This author wonders what would have been the effect on the budget and U.S. economic growth if the public deficit was reduced by slightly over one half due to the aborted lives living and contributing these tax revenues.

Each aborted life would have also consumed some federal and state revenue via goods and services consumed by public school services, public transportation, public safety or law enforcement, etc.. But this might be offset by the tax income generated by goods, and services purchased by the aborted lives; unemployment insurance taxes and business taxes collected by businesses employing these lives; and the production of goods and services from these aborted lives.

One other important point is that estimated tax revenue loss will increase as taxation levels increase in the U.S. and as the cumulative number of abortions increase. What do I mean by this statement? If the aborted lives had lived and aged, their income and tax revenues would have increased. Also, as federal taxation levels increase (just compare the percentage of average federal tax revenue collected for 1973 versus 1993), more tax revenue is NOT collected from the aborted lives. Simply put, a 1973 life (aborted) would have produced increased tax revenues (i.e. upon entering higher tax brackets) in its 30's (starting in the year 2003) and 40's (starting in the year 2013). The cumulative effect of these lost lives will be increasingly felt as the U.S. enters the 21st Century. As more abortions occur, the effect of cumulative abortions will increase

as  more consumers and laborers are "missing" from the tax
revenue system.

In conclusion, although the data is still "young"
chronologically for the aborted lives, as the cumulative
abortions continues to age (AND cumulative abortions
increase), it will become increasingly clear that a section  of
potential tax revenues will be missing. This may  contribute
to the increasing U.S. public deficit and  subsequent U.S. public
debt.  Over time this "lost"  income may also be detected in
lost Social Security revenues, perhaps adding to the financial
strain of the Social Security system as the U.S. population
ages  and enters onto social security retirement rolls.

# CHAPTER 10
## LONG RANGE EFFECTS
## OF ABORTION

This chapter explores several effects of abortion that will occur in other arenas of society. These effects will not be easily detected until the late 1990's or early 21st Century (e.g. 2010-2020). For those seeking topics for long term research projects, follow several of these topics until the year 2025, and perhaps follow up with a book of your own!

As time progresses, the cumulative effects of abortion will be felt in many segments of society. Even if ALL abortions ended today, the cumulative effects of over 20 years of abortions would be felt for many decades to come.

The impact of abortion on education will be eventually demonstrated in further decreases in teacher job availability, decreased numbers of candidates for associate, bachelor, masters, and Ph.D. degrees, decreased property tax revenues, further decreases in economic growth, decreased housing starts, decreased industrial productivity (YES, even decreased toy manufacturing!), and decreased federal and state fiscal stability due to decreases in income tax and Social Security revenues. This last difficulty may contribute to further Social Security retirement fund solvency problems, especially in the early 21st century, as a larger segment of the U.S. population (i.e. the baby boomers) enters into retirement age (28).

THE COST OF ABORTION

Another example of the future effect of abortion involves new home purchases. New housing purchases will suffer declines by 2005-2015. If the average age of new home buyers remains at about 30 (29), then the cost of abortion will begin to be felt by 2003-2005. Furthermore, as abortions decrease fertility of women who obtain abortions and generally decrease the U.S. total fertility rate, then first time home buyer data will continue to show a statistical decline in family size.

A Department of Commerce study (29) of first time home owners states that more first time home buyers had no children in 1989 (56%) than in 1977 (49%)(see Graph 10.1).

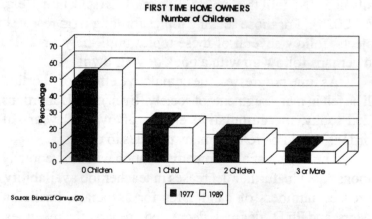

**GRAPH 10.1** - FIRST TIME HOME PURCHASES FOR 1977 AND 1989; AMOUNT OF CHILDREN.

Data on first time home buyers with 1, 2, and 3 or more children for 1989 demonstrated a similar decline when compared with 1977 data. This may be due in part to abortion. Repeat studies of these statistics every 5 years may add support to this supposition.

66

Also, as the U.S. population ages and the cumulative effects of abortion increase, first time home buyers in 2010 or 2020 will be younger (or older depending on prevailing wages), have less children, but find housing costs reduced (compared to the late 1980's). This may be due to reduced demand (i.e. market competition) because of a decline in available buyers, another cost of abortion! Consider, also, the effects that a reduction of new housing construction will have on the construction related jobs of masons, lumberjacks, carpenters, electricians, etc.

Finally, the cost of abortion will affect national security. It may be difficult to believe, but as the cumulative effects of abortion manifest themselves the capacity of the U.S. to recruit and finance sufficient numbers of young people for military service (peace time or war time) will be in jeopardy. If the U.S. can not muster sufficient troop strength, our capacity to meet foreign aggressors will decline. Wattenberg (30) clarifies the effect of decreased birth rate on military strength and national security. He states that a superpower requires BOTH high technology AND a large population to maintain its superpower status. A robust population is necessary, not to only field a military, but to support the military with a strong industrial production capability, a competent scientific and engineering staff, and to provide a transportation network to sustain supplies and communication.

Consider the following rapid mental exercise to comprehend the need for a strong population for U.S. military security: Picture the numbers of construction personnel, scientists, engineers, transportation personnel, military training specialists, and raw material suppliers, that are required to design, build, supply, maintain, and train for such military necessities as aircraft carriers, spy satellites, air cargo carriers like the C-5 and/or C-17, nuclear submarines or a battalion of M-1 tanks or a Patriot missile battery.

Since abortion contributes to declining birth rates and to declining total fertility rates, then the cost of abortion may include effects on military strength and national security. To our horror, the coming decade may show evidence of this last point.

# CHAPTER 11
# CONCLUSIONS

Although legally induced abortions have been a protected right for about 20 years, the long-term social and economic effects of abortion are just now beginning to manifest themselves. The clearest evidence of the cost of abortion is in the areas of adoptions, fertility rates, education (especially teacher employment), population growth, and GDP and personal income growth. Some factors could have hidden or extraneous variables (e.g. contraception use, homosexuality, more working women, economic recessions, etc.) that do not lend themselves to easy cause and effect conclusions, However, I believe that the clearest effects of abortion are seen in adoptions, fertility rates, and education/teacher employment positions.

BUT, the effects do not stop there. The cost of abortion will become clearly seen in other social and economic arenas. These may include economic growth, housing starts, military strength and national security, and stability of the social security system.

Also, I suspect other (as yet unseen) medical problems will surface for women that have obtained abortions. Like Asherman's Syndrome, these disorders will not always be easy to diagnose nor will clinical studies sufficiently describe the epidemiological scope of the disorder. These problems may be further complicated if the disorders are swept up into the miasma of "abortion political correctness" and pro-choice rhetoric, rather than discussed in the clinical light of scientific thought. Sadly, the women who obtained abortions will be victimized for a second time (the first time was by undergoing the abortion) and silently suffer, along with society, in ignorance.

Perhaps a review of these studies in 5 and 10 years will reinforce these conclusions and provide significant arguments for an end to abortion in the United States. These later studies will probably concur with this study: that legal induced abortions have had a deleterious effect on select social, economic, and demographic aspects of American society. The cost of abortion affects all of us.

# AFTERWORD

Mr. Roberge's work <u>The Cost Of Abortion</u> highlights a difficult issue in scholarship and in research. How to study the 'unrecorded event'? The cost of abortion has been commented upon by some demographers obliquely and by moralists directly. However, as in research on the History of Plagues, it is the 'non-event' or the 'assumed event' that can be impossible to ferret out with any degree of absolute certainty. Moreover, if the event is unpopular, distasteful, or embarrassing, collective <u>scotoma</u> occurs and the subconscious process of "collective denial" allows the phenomenon to blend into the background of common but unspecified knowledge. David Horowitz did this with <u>The Destructive Generation</u> and Lawrence Roberge has attempted it with this work.

Education, medicine, geriatrics, law, and social policy and social activism have all been changed by Roe vs. Wade and the society that demanded it as a 'rite of passage'.

The impact of abortion as a social policy of preference on our families, our care of our children, our elders, ourselves is still being unpacked in the society around us. The slopes of human endeavor are indeed slippery, but especially so when we ignore the world that could have been as well as the world that has become us. But, the story of contemporary social policy and moral temperament cannot be completed without a serious look at the world that Mr. Roberge has begun to point out to us.

If this is the age of discovery of 'new paradigms' and new methods of comparison, then Mr. Roberge's research deserves honest review and comment. In a fashion similar to the work of Henry Hobhouse in The Forces of Change (Little, Brown), Mr. Roberge has highlighted the details of social policy decisions in the most dramatic form. Certainly, upper class Americans and even middle class Americans can engage in the cat and mouse game of denial that marks the epitome of arrogance of our time, but the staggering numbers that are impacted in the social projections elucidated by Mr. Roberge cry out for scrutiny and examination. Sadly, as in the denial of the Holocaust, it is incredibly difficult to get Americans to focus on their own holocaust and to face the fact that they may be on the verge of creating an even greater one for the next generation.

By definition, the final study of the topic cannot be completed and the definitive work will always be in the making. Yet, Mr. Roberge has begun a path of reflection and analysis that may define the pathways that led us from 1984 to someone's Brave New World. This world will be populated, but not by all who might have been there had some of us seen the real results of our decisions after "1973".

James McGregor
Associate Professor
Salem State College
Salem, Massachusetts

# BIBLIOGRAPHY

1-Limbaugh, R. 1992, The Way Things Ought to Be. New York, Pocket Books.

2-Flanders, C.N. 1991, Abortion. New York, Facts on File.

3-Centers for Disease Control and Prevention, Abortion Surveillance, In: CDC Surveillance Summaries, September 4, 1992, MMWR 1992; 4 (No:33-5): 1-34

4-Henshaw, S., van Hort, J., ed. 1992 Abortion Fact Book 1992. New York, The Alan Guttmacher Institute.

5-Henshaw, S.K., van Hort, J., Abortion Services in the United States, 1987 and 1988. Fam Plann Perspect. 22, 3, May/June 1990, p 102-108, 142

6-Westoff, C. F., Fertility in the United States, Science, 234, 4776, Oct 1986, p 554-559

7-The Rise in Births is Only an Echo of the Baby Boom, Business Week, 3114, July 10, 1989, p 18

8-New Boom; No Panic, The New York Times, Dec 9, 1990, p 16

9-Wattenberg, B.J. 1987, The Birth Dearth. New York, Pharos

Books.

10-Wattenberg, B. J., ibid, p 124

11-Huggins, G.R., Cullins, V.E., Fertility After Contraception or Abortion, Fertil Steril. 54, 4, Oct 1990, p 559-573

12-Tricopoulos, D., Handanos, N., Danezis, J., Kalandidi, A., Kalapothaki, V., Induced Abortion and Secondary Infertility. Br. J. Obstet Gyn. 83, 1976, p 645-650

13-Hogue, C.J.R., Cates, W., Tietze, C., Impact of Vacuum Aspiration Abortion on Future Childbearing: A Review. Fam Plann Perspect. 15, 3, 1983, p 119-126

14-Daling, J.R., Emanuel, I., Induced Abortion and Subsequent Outcome of Pregnancy in a Series of American Women. New Eng. J. Med. 297, 23, 1977, p 1241-1245

15-Koop, C.E., A Measured Response: Koop on Abortion. Fam Plann Perspect. 21, 1989, p 31

16-Klein, S.M., Garcia, C.R., Asherman's Syndrome: A Critique and Current Review. Fertil Steril. 24, 9, 1973, p 722-735

17-Ismajovich, B., Lidor, A., Confino, E., David, M.P., Treatment of Minimal and Moderate Intrauterine Adhesions (Asherman's Syndrome), J. Reprod. Med. 30, 10, 1985, p 769- 772

18-March, C.M., Israel, R., Intrauterine Adhesions Secondary to Elective Abortion. Obstet Gynecol. 48, 4, 1976, p 422-424

19-Henshaw, S.K., Koonin, L.M., Smith, J.C., Characteristics of U.S. Women Having Abortions, 1987. Fam Plann Perspect. 23, 2, 1991, p 75-81

20-Adoption Fact Book June 1989, Washington, DC, National Council for Adoption.

21-Atrash, H.K., Lawson, H.W., Smith, J.C., Legal Abortion in the U.S.: Trends and Mortality. Contemp Ob/Gyn. 35, Feb 1990, p 58-69

22-Wattenberg, B.J., op cit., p 29-30 and p 165.

23-ibid p 23-24

24-ibid p 7

25-The 1993-94 Resolutions of the National Education Association, NEA Today, 12, 2, Septemeber 1993, p 25-35

26-Garland, S.B., How the Abortion Issue is Shaking the House of Labor, Business Week, Aug 6, 1990, p 39

27-Internal Revenue Service; Statistics of Income Bulletin; Spring 1993, Washington, DC, 1993 p 136

28-Wattenberg, B.J., op cit., p 65

29-U.S. Bureau of the Census, Current Housing Report, H121/

93-1, First-Time Homeowners in 1989: A Comparative Perspective, U.S. Government Printing Office, Washington, DC, 1993

30-Wattenberg, B.J., op cit., p 38, 88-99

31-Kuhar, B.M., 1993, Abortifacient Drugs and Devices, Ingomar, PA, Kuhar Konsultants.

32-Farhi, J., Bar-Hava, I., Homburg, R., Dicker, D., Ben-Rafael, Z., Induced Regeneration of Endometrium Following Curettage for Abortion: A Comparative Study. Hum. Reprod., 8, 7, 1993, p 1143-1144

33-Shigawa, S., Nagayama, M., Cervical Pregnancy as a Possible Sequela of Induced Abortion. Report of 19 Cases., Am. J. Obst. & Gynec., 105, 2, 1969, p 282-284

34-Dicker, D., Feldberg, D., Samuel, N., Goldman, J.A., Etiology of Cervical Pregnancy: Association with Abortion, Pelvic Pathology, IUDs, and Asherman's Syndrome. J. Reprod. Med., 30, 1, 1985, p 25-27

35-Glendon, M.A., 1987, Abortion and Divorce in Western Law. Cambridge, Harvard University Press.

36-An Italian Irony: The Land That is Home to Papacy Boasts Planet's Lowest Birthrate, The Christian Science Monitor, Aug 13, 1993, p 1, 4

37-Italy Birth Rate Hits Record Low, The Boston Globe, July 31, 1994, p 13

38-Thomas, C., Clinic Violence Not Justifiable, The Springfield Union-News, Jan 12, 1995

39-Henshaw, S.K., Van Vort, J., Abortion Services in the United States, 1991 and 1992., Fam Plann Perspect., 26, 1994, 100-106 & 112

40-[Koonin, L. M., Smith, J.C., Ramick, M.:][Abortion Surveillance-United States, 1990] IN: CDC Surveillance Summaries. Dec 17, 1993. MMWR 1993; 42 (no. SS-6): [29-57].

41-1992 Graves, E.G., Detailed Diagnosis and Procedures, National Hospital Discharge Survey, 1992. National Center for Health Statistics. Vital Health Stat. 13 (118). 1994.

42-1991 Graves, E.G., Detailed Diagnosis and Procedures, National Hospital Discharge Survey, 1991. National Center for Health Statistics. Vital Health Stat. 13 (115). 1993.

43-1990 Graves, E.G., Detailed Diagnosis and Procedures, National Hospital Discharge Survey, 1990. National Center for Health Statistics. Vital Health Stat. 13 (108). 1991.

44-1989 Graves, E.G., Detailed Diagnosis and Procedures, National Hospital Discharge Survey, 1989. National Center for Health Statistics. Vital Health Stat. 13 (108). 1991.

45-1988 Graves, E.G., Detailed Diagnosis and Procedures, National Hospital Discharge Survey, 1988. National Center for Health Statistics. Vital Health Stat. 13 (107). 1991.

46-Montalbano, W.D.,  Italian's Baby Boom Goes Bust, The Los Angeles Times, June 24, 1994,  A1 + A6.